S0-FJC-812

Library of
Davidson College

VOID

Library of
Davidson College

Transforming
the
American
Garden:
12
New
Landscape
Designs

Michael R. Van Valkenburgh
Associate Professor of
Landscape Architecture


Margaret B. Reeve
Curator of Exhibitions

Jory Johnson
Curatorial Assistant

Harvard
University
Graduate
School
of
Design

712.6
V284t

86-4309

Copyright © 1986 by Michael R. Van Valkenburgh. All rights reserved. No part of this publication may be reproduced without written permission of the author. Published by Harvard University Graduate School of Design, Cambridge, MA. Printed in the United States of America.

Library of Congress Catalog Card Number: 86-373
International Standard Book Number: 0-935617-02-7

Copies of *Transforming the American Garden: 12 New Landscape Designs* are available for purchase from the Office of Special Programs, Harvard University Graduate School of Design, 48 Quincy Street, Cambridge, MA 02138. 617-495-9340

Design: Barbara Stauffacher Solomon. Mechanical art: Mary Reilly. Typesetter: Monotype Composition, Inc., Boston. Typeface: Bodoni. Printer: Reynolds-DeWalt, New Bedford, MA. Photography: Charles Mayer, 5000K, Boston. Production: Communications Office, Harvard University Graduate School of Design.

Cover: Detail, Barbara Stauffacher Solomon, 2 Fields + 3 Houses = A Landscape

Acknowledgments

The catalogue was
published in connection
with the exhibition
"Transforming the
American Garden:
12 New Landscape
Designs" sponsored by
Harvard University
Graduate School of
Design; the Design Arts
Program of the National
Endowment for the
Arts, a Federal Agency
in Washington, D.C.;
and the New England
Foundation for the
Arts, a consortium of
the six New England
state arts agencies.

The catalogue was
supported by a grant
from the Graham
Foundation for
Advanced Studies in
the Fine Arts.

Additional funding
was provided by:
the New England
Foundation for the
Arts, a consortium of
the six New England
state arts agencies; the
Daniel Urban Kiley
Lectures & Exhibitions
Fund of Harvard
University Graduate
School of Design;
The Architectural
League of New York; the
National Endowment
for the Arts, a Federal
Agency in Washington,
D.C.; Landscape Forms,
Inc., Kalamazoo, MI;
State Street Bank &
Trust Company, Boston;
and William H.
Frederick, Jr.

Exhibition Dates:

The Architectural
League of New York:
February 17–March 14,
1986

Harvard University
Graduate School of
Design: April 1–18, 1986

State Street Bank &
Trust Company, Boston:
April 20–June 20, 1986

The exhibition will tour
through December 1987
under the auspices of
the New England
Foundation for the
Arts.

Other sites will include
the University of
California at Berkeley,
Fall 1986, and The Otis
Art Institute of Parsons
School of Design, Los
Angeles, Fall 1986.

# Table of Contents

Gardens embody the essence of landscape architecture. Like architects' designs for houses, garden designs are succinct and expressive statements. In this century, the garden has provided a subject for developing design ideas which formulated later inquiries in other settings. For example, Lawrence Halprin's investigations of water in the McIntyre Garden in California contributed significantly, a decade later, to his design of the remarkable Auditorium Forecourt fountain in Portland, Oregon.

The purpose of *Transforming the American Garden: 12 New Landscape Designs* is to illuminate ideas about design by a group of younger landscape architects currently practicing in the United States. Work on this exhibition began three years ago, when I discovered an essay by Fletcher Steele in *Contemporary Landscape Architecture and Its Sources*, an exhibition catalogue produced in 1937 by the San Francisco Museum of Art and funded in part by the Federal Art Project. Steele's essay outlined the issues that concerned the designers in that exhibition, and this provided me with a clearer understanding of that period in landscape design history. It occurred to me that the field of landscape architecture might benefit from a new set of design inquiries that paralleled the efforts of our predecessors fifty years ago to capture the spirit of their era.

The early stages of this project were funded by a National Endowment for the Arts Design Exploration Grant. Nominations of possible participants were sought, with the stipulation that those nominated should be early or mid-career American landscape architects with demonstrated expertise in garden design. It was essential that the participants define themselves as landscape architects, thus eliminating artists who work with landscape and architects who make gardens. Some of their work is provocative and could be the subject of another exhibition.

The final guidelines for the entries in this exhibition resulted from suggestions by each of the participants. Jory Johnson and I circulated preliminary guidelines to the participants for comments and revisions. The designers agreed that each design would address the flower as a design element. The sites, either public or private, would be individually selected and approximately one acre in size. Most participants chose to work with a site in their own geographic region.

Each of the twelve entries was conceived as an ideal garden, embracing a personal philosophy. Out of this inventive spirit a variety of designs and accompanying statements have emerged, expressing the range of thinking about garden design today. Without actual clients, the proposed gardens are speculative and conceptual. Obviously, many of the proposals would change in interaction with clients. Each proposal suggests ideas that, if tested by pragmatic concerns such as a budget, could formulate or direct the selection of alternatives. Gardens evolve in complex ways, not singularly from practical constraints, but from an artistic vision that guides the particular manner in which practical concerns are resolved.

Conceptualizing designs is distinct from making things. Ideas spring from our hearts and minds and are informed by history and culture and tempered with a keen knowledge of how the world is built. Designing a garden is an artistic activity; making a landscape is a craft. Great gardens are the physical manifestation of both. This synthesis, at times mysterious, defines creativity in landscape architecture.

Michael Van Valkenburgh

Garden design is a transformation of nature into a visionary and symbolic expression; it is not merely an ordering of plants within a described boundary, which might be termed landscaping. Parks, larger landscapes and even most backyards are shaped by an accrual of artifacts and interventions such as roads, buildings, playing fields and monuments. They are a collective expression of popular culture, while a garden is a singular expression. This is more a critical judgment than a definition, but it is important to realize that a garden can be a very public place. Gardens are distinctive not for their private nature, but for the designer's intention.

What, then, is an American garden? Like architecture, gardens in the United States during the 18th and 19th centuries were strongly influenced by European models. Often, they were copies of European gardens with little regard for their context or meaning. In the 20th century, this eclectic borrowing broadened to include Japanese references, as well as the abstraction of functional forms from nature. American garden design has not been widely regarded either as a fine art worthy of serious investigation and critical analysis or as fertile ground for psychological and metaphysical speculation. By describing the garden in subcategories such as walks, groundcovers and walls, many garden publications have reduced the idea of the garden to a combination of ingredients which provide comfort, function and horticultural display.

Any meaningful discussion of the American garden must address the American landscape. In the nation's early days, the Edenic wonder and transcendence of its unspoiled beauty lured the painters of the Hudson River and Luminist schools with images of primal creation. In their vast canvases, man is a tiny spectator. Americans, however, soon learned to domesticate this majestic landscape. The wilderness was tamed through celebration of anomalies such as New Hampshire's Old Man of the Mountain, or by framing photo opportunities of the Grand Canyon and other scenic wonders. Today, the grandest views of Niagara Falls are so enshrined in popular culture that they can never again inspire the awe captured in Frederick Edwin Church's paintings. For the designers in this exhibition, a field of California poppies, a row of Siberian iris or a tangle of chaparral have become symbols of the formerly sacred and sublime landscape. It is no longer the spectacle of Niagara Falls but the daily ebb and flow of a Miami tide that embodies the spiritual essence of nature.

Many of the participants in the exhibition, free to invent their site and context, produced designs which exemplify a strong response to ecology and regional culture. But they do more than mimic motifs or regional styles: they transform aspects or emblems of the regional landscape into gardens where one can make spiritual connections to one's native culture and values. The gardens are not only sited along the Virginia coast or on a Midwestern farm, for example, but also express the "bonded humanity" of Virginia's past and present, or the independent, practical nature of the Illinois farmer.

The range and diversity of its sources make it difficult to define the American garden. At the same time, these are the very qualities which make the garden a provocative field for artistic exploration today. Americans are not beholden to the almost oppressive traditions of Europe. At the same time, the diversity and vigor of this country's heritage grants its designers the freedom to borrow from sources as widespread as Sufi mysticism and Pop Art. But if the American garden does not really exist as a single, identifiable history. A prominent example of a narrative and symbolic garden is Henry Hoare Stourhead, built in England in the 18th century. Hoare lost many members of his family through illness and tragic accidents, and sought to express his sense of despair and rejuvenation by constructing a symbolic journey in his garden. He tried to universalize his private sorrow through classical allusions to Aeneas's journey to the underworld in search of his dead father and through the sensory experiences of his garden.

Many of these twelve designers describe their gardens through a similar narrative of its parts, confident that one would find the emotional experience of their garden's intention compelling.

form, how can it be transformed? The twelve designers in this exhibition do not invent new forms, but revise traditional garden elements such as bosques, hedges and fountains to formulate designs with new content and meaning. The transformation of gardens from eclectic ensembles to cohesive, legible designs is the underlying theme of this exhibition.

There are many precedents for symbolic expression in garden

Henry Hoare's vision, as expressed at Stourhead, was not as strong an influence on American garden design as that of his compatriot and contemporary, Capability Brown. Brown's gardens, devoid of classical allusions and Claudian motifs, did not express philosophical ideas about the landscape, but rather exploited the "capabilities" of a site to yield a pleasing composition of trees, fields and water. Long before architecture was shorn

of ornamentation and classical orders, Western gardens, partially through Brown's influence, had become abstract compositions of self-referential forms. Yet designs in this exhibition, like Henry Hoare's, reflect an interest in symbolic expression rather than in the lure of abstraction.

From the time a shaman stood in front of a cave painting and recited the myth or tale that inspired it, words have been a necessary part of art. In America, gardens have been impoverished by a denial of meaning in favor of an emphasis on craft. The personal statements of each designer in the exhibition are part of a vital effort now emerging to develop a theoretical context for landscape architecture.

By examining old assumptions and offering new challenges, these designers have expanded the scope of the American garden. But the garden can only hold ideas which can be expressed in physical form. Once inside a garden, we are caught in the immediacy of the experience. We can never react dispassionately and intellectually, and one problematic aspect of any design exhibition is the effort required to imagine oneself within these gardens, experiencing them spatially from dawn to

dusk. To assist in this task, the catalogue is ordered geographically; we travel from the East to the West coast through these speculations. The designs all strive to create an American garden capable of embodying a sense of ourselves. If they are to succeed, these gardens must be part of a larger order of meaning as well as significant guides to the future of American gardens.

Jory Johnson

"So that all the designs will have a common starting point for discussion, your landscape should address the flower in some way. We chose this theme because built landscapes and gardens could not exist today without the ability of man to use plants as an artistic medium. The fields and forests of flowering plants were the landscape until man transformed it. It should not be viewed as a 'flower garden,' but as an uncompromising examination of the sources of landscape design. Since flowering plants have been a subject of all art forms (structures and morphology as well as blossoms), the flower should be inspiration for new directions and ideas.

"The flower has aroused an astonishing gamut of emotional and philosophical responses, and is a propitious point of origin for your design. Be it cultivated or wild, sculptured or organic, on trees or on annuals in pots, the flower must have a place in your garden. Obviously, your consideration of the flower will serve as a springboard for a discussion of the eternal questions facing any garden designer: man's relationship to nature, his role on the earth, and his hopes, fears and dreams of the future."

The 12 Landscape Designs

sional drifter sleeping off a drunk) by traversing a hundred yards of terrifying and exhilarating forest. Who can say if any Road adventure has been manifest in my work, but I sometimes wonder if my can of buried pennies ever became some other kid's miraculous discovery.

A friend who lives in a Korean Buddhist monastery writes, "There aren't any gardens in America anymore." And I think I agree with him, at least in the sense of garden-as-paradise. It wouldn't be so verbalized, but everyone seems to believe that they can/should/ must make use of somebody else's paradise as their own.

anyone anymore. Even Hilton Kramer knows: "That the culture (Picasso) set out to attack and transform proved to be more resilient in its response to this assault than anyone at the time had reason to expect; that it showed itself capable of absorbing such assaults and profitting from them —this, I should have thought, would now, in the next to last decade of the twentieth century, have become an acknowledged datum of critical intelligence." No, we may not be able to shock them anymore, but the audience double-dares us to try, and then books the place for the Debutante Ball. What *is* a designer to do?

"Burial in a sacred grove is an ancient privilege."
Paul Shepard

Oh, don't talk to me about gardens and spatial poetics, *A la recherche du temps perdu* and paradise. The only paradise, as Richard Ellman says, is the one that has been lost. Who do you know who has made it all the way to *Within a Budding Grove*?

Where I grew up we had the "Old Back Road." You got to The Road (a foreign-country-in-the-suburbs complete with abandoned farmhouse, snakes and an occa-

Yeah, it's a sign of the times that most designers don't perceive the signs of the times (or are unable to make use of this perception if they do). But since when is that new? Lacking vision or insight or courage, steal somebody else's. However, one person's vision is another's vertigo; insight— insanity; and courage, well, call me collect if you find any. One thing I do know, it doesn't spring parthenogenetically from freestanding walls painted primary colors.

Yes, today's predicament is a bit more perplexing than Venturi's in '66. We can't shock

But maybe I'm wrong. Maybe Bob did his job *too* well. Maybe designers are *too* perceptive. If Barthes is right that what distinguishes so-called advanced societies from those of the past is that they consume images rather than beliefs, then all those purloined pillars are just what the public ordered.

In such light, this project—a private cemetery —flies in the face of the contemporary. For what aspect of human experience is more saturated with notorious and blindly-held beliefs than death? You might say that this garden offers the opportunity

to employ one's beliefs or to have their absence exposed.

You'll want to know that Valanakis's *Oedipus* was researched and that the labyrinth is of Pima origin. Sure, at one time or another we've all coveted the artist's secret code. But don't express intentions compromise your response? Perhaps we need to decide if Duchamp was right when he said that the most important thing about a painting is its title.

The cubes are clipped horsechestnuts; the pavilions trained and clipped yews.

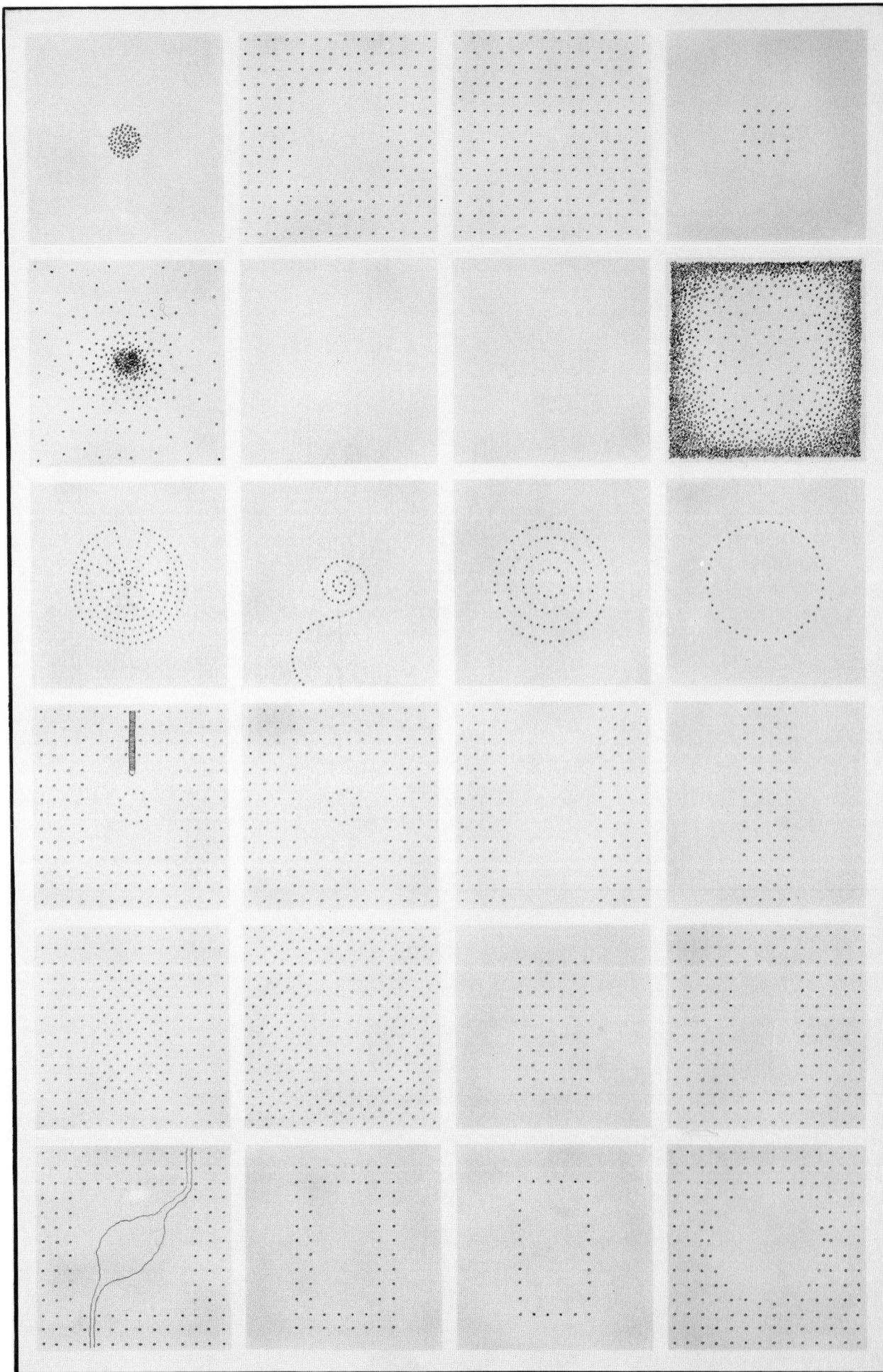

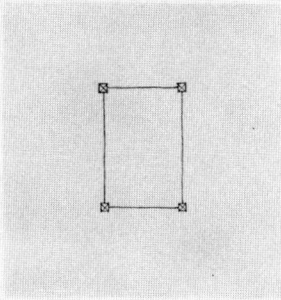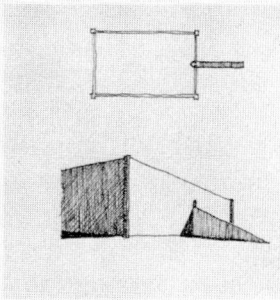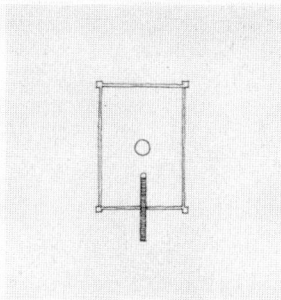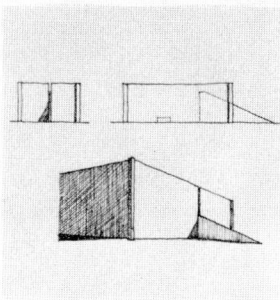
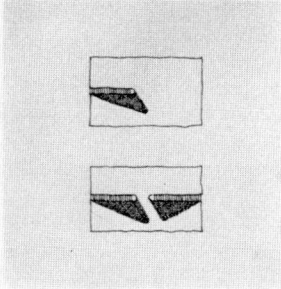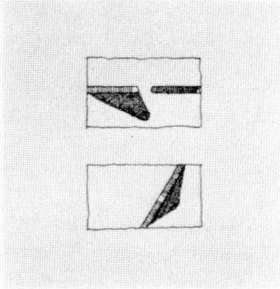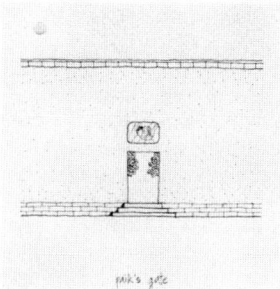
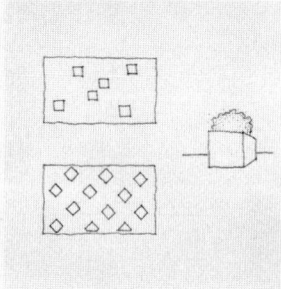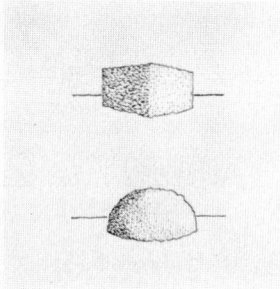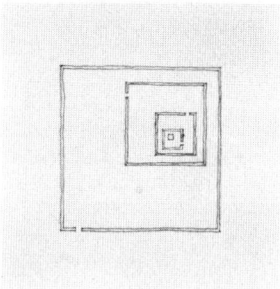

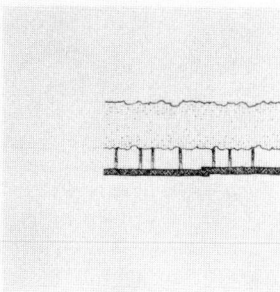
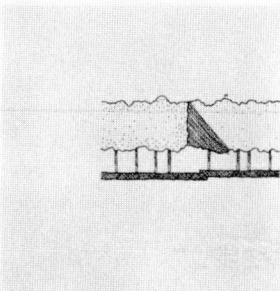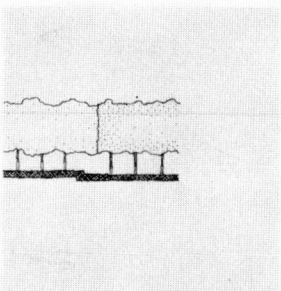

Martha Schwartz

The New York City Bulb Garden

Problem: The site is an 86-by-23-foot roof on top of a six-story building in Manhattan's SoHo district. One enters the space through a small building at the east end—a living room attached to the loft space below—and by a stairwell from the west end.

The garden must be durable, easy to maintain and lightweight. The feeling of great space and openness, so precious to New York living, should be emphasized. The garden should also incorporate the elements of seasonal change, color and movement.

Solution: A large planting bed (19-by-62-feet) has been built up from the existing roof surface. This bed is 18 inches deep and is contained at the east and west ends by three steps, and at the south by a four-foot-wide path. The masonry is concrete block covered with an asphalt-based roofing compound. Visually, it will link the new construction to the existing roof's vernacular.

This planting bed will be filled first with 2 inches of gravel for drainage, 12 inches of lightweight soil mix, and will be topped with 4 inches of sand. It will contain 4,712 6-inch clay pots, each pot containing one of four different species of bulbs. These pots will be placed in the planting bed according to a planting plan for each species. In order to properly place the bulbs, each pot and bulb has a specific number that places it within a numbered grid. Once the pots are placed, a specific pot in this garden can be located by finding the pot's coordinate numbers and letters (stenciled upon the walls and on the top steps) and then locating their point of intersection.

The bulbs selected for this scheme are daffodils, Greek anemone, Peruvian lily and hardy amaryllis. They bloom respectively in spring, summer, early fall and late fall. The bulbs have been selected for their low maintenance requirements and their ability to withstand frost and freezing temperatures.

The system is designed for flexibility. Bulbs can be replaced and new planting plans can be easily implemented.

The garden can be irrigated with a garden hose.

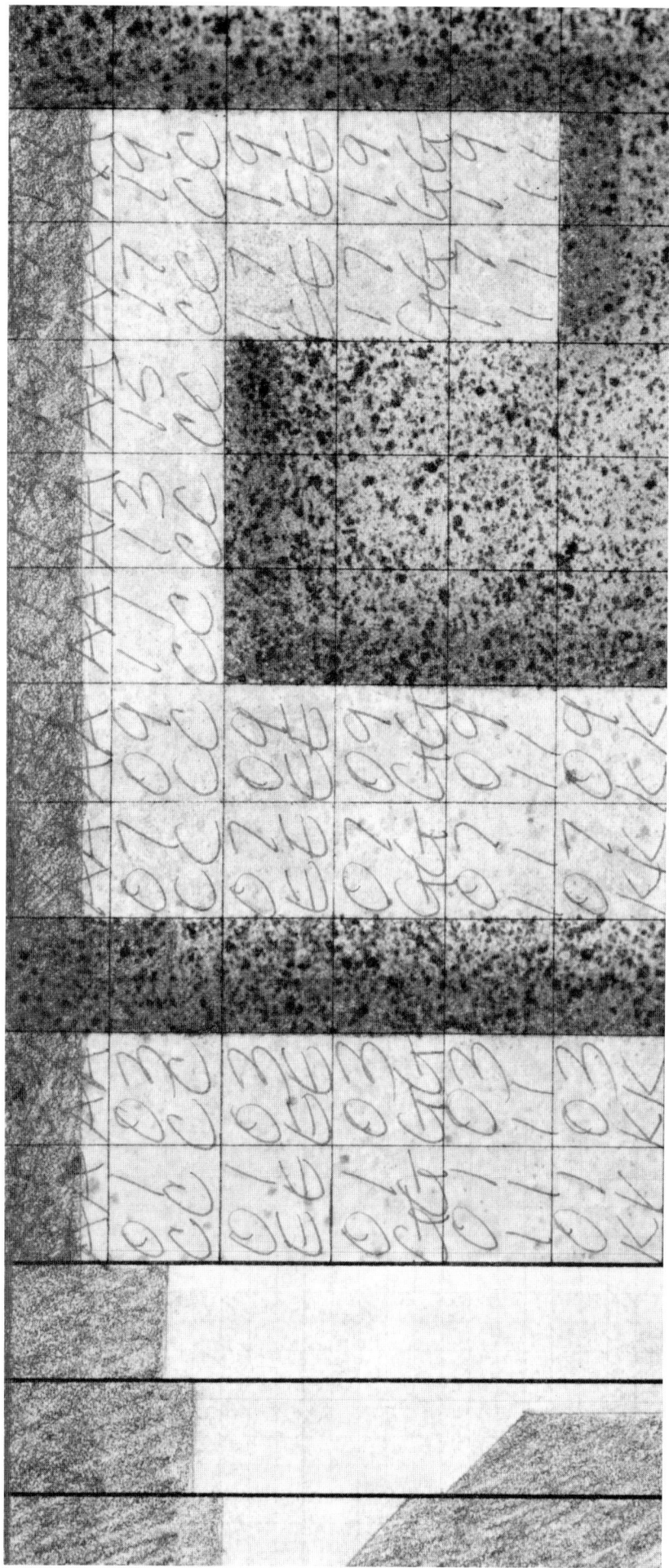

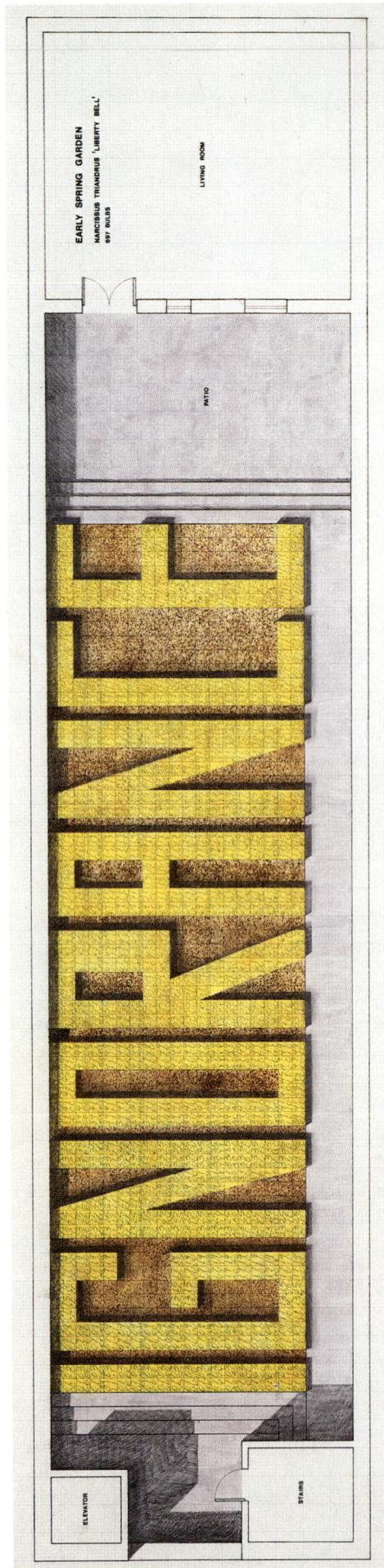

**EARLY SPRING GARDEN**
NARCISSUS TRIANDRUS 'LIBERTY BELL'
897 BULBS

LIVING ROOM

PATIO

IGNORANCE

ELEVATOR

STAIRS

**SUMMER GARDEN**
ANEMONE BLANDA
GREEK ANEMONE
595 BULBS

LIVING ROOM

PATIO

EVIL

ELEVATOR

STAIRS

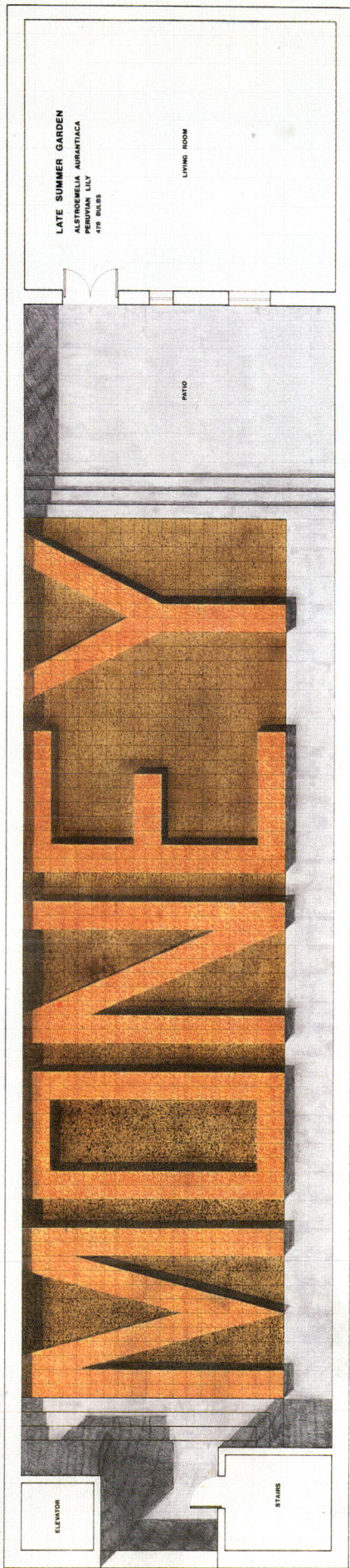

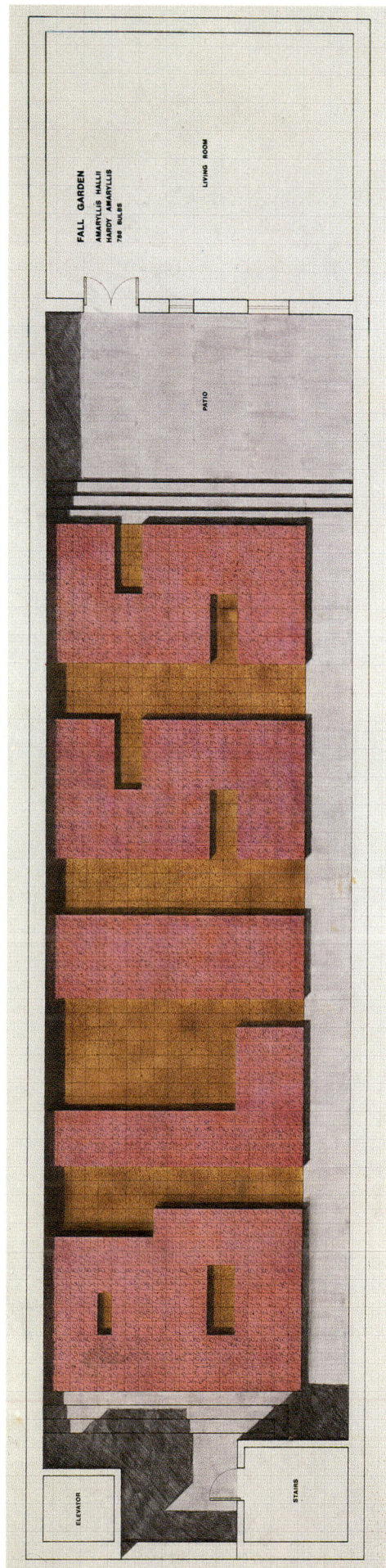

LATE SUMMER GARDEN

ALSTROEMELIA AURANTIACA
PERUVIAN LILY
475 BULBS

LIVING ROOM

PATIO

ELEVATOR

STAIRS

FALL GARDEN

AMARYLLIS HALLI
HARDY AMARYLLIS
750 BULBS

LIVING ROOM

PATIO

ELEVATOR

STAIRS

Michael R. Van
Valkenburgh

Eudoxia: A New
Civic Landscape

Eudoxia is guided by my conviction that landscape design is both personally expressive and socially motivated. I believe that any design idea requires an interpretation of its formal precedents and natural processes, whether or not these are explicit in the final design. Inspiration for imagery arises from these and other, unsuspected sources—dreams, fleeting thoughts, memories.

Architecture and landscape architecture share the task of making functional and memorable places. Yet landscapes are open to the sky. Without a differentiation between inside and out, a landscape must be judged in spatial *and* sculptural terms. Indeed, this paradox is ubiquitous to the field and is a central concern explored in this project.

The name Eudoxia is taken from Italo Calvino's *Invisible Cities*, which, in its vision of the city, prompted this proposal. I was particularly taken with the following passage:

"An oracle was questioned about the mysterious bond between two objects so dissimilar as the carpet and the city. One of the two objects—the oracle replied—has the form the gods gave the starry sky and the orbits in which the worlds revolve; the other is an approximate reflection, like every human creation."

The garden proposed here is a rich, woven, dense landscape like Calvino's imaginary carpet that captures a city's essence. Calibrated in its forms, exacting in its intent, Eudoxia is not a scenic landscape but a scenography for contemporary life.

This garden is intended for an urban, corporate headquarters and is located between a pair of new, three-story buildings. The garden cuts through an entire city block with street frontage at the north and south ends. It provides ceremonial entrances and places for meeting and contemplation, and is open to the public.

Eudoxia's composition is in the spirit of early 20th century modernists: abstracted geometric forms and spaces are linked by a broken axis and are balanced by proportion rather than symmetry. Influences include Cubism and the paintings of Moholy-Nagy. The hedge composition departs from the machine aesthetic of the modernists in the organicism of its materials and reliance on the seasonally changing color matrix of a palette of deciduous plants. Hedges derive from the typology of planted forms by Lutyens and Jekyll and from Vita Sackville-West's Sissinghurst. Embodying a new landscape type, Eudoxia uses elements of private gardens while relating to the city in scale and complexity.

The garden joins an urban exterior to an intimate interior. Beginning at the south end, an arc of trees bows over the sidewalk edge to establish a landscape stylobate inviting entry. A twelve-foot stucco screen wall, set back from the sidewalk, is reiterated in a parallel evergreen hedge. Windows in the wall and hedge frame the landscape composition within and two doorways frame the major entry points.

The building entrances are located at the street ends under continuous, double-story loggias that extend the length of the buildings at the east and west sides, establishing covered passageways from the buildings and the garden. A labyrinth of corridors formed by hedges offers a series of pathways between the two buildings. Users of the garden may revise their daily walks to include different plant fragrances, colors and densities. Each hedge is composed of one plant species. Some are evergreen, others deciduous; some have unpruned tops, others have a finished surface. A sixteen-foot-high, circular purple beech hedge is lodged asymmetrically within the composition and is incised by lowering the ground level five steps. From the ground, it is seen as a vanishing ellipse. Viewed from above, the hedge composition functions as a large parterre. Along each loggia, hedge niches provide sites for sculpture and offer places for conversation or rest.

Near the center of the garden, isolated in a narrow room, is a long, raised herbaceous border of blue-flowered Siberian Iris. The image is inspired by Rothko's paintings, but here the tonality responds to seasonal light rather than the edge of the canvas. In November the withered brown foliage tacitly anticipates the stark beauty of winter.

Beyond the flower border, pressed deep into the earth, is a court of stone and water. Eleven water trays, filmed with water and separated by paths, are cut into the center. Each tray empties into a main pool at the base of a gently curved, twenty-five-foot-high wall of rock, bound at each side by cut stone pillars. Water pipes—like those found in cleft rock springs—pierce the wall at the top, pouring water in summer and accumulating ice in winter. The ice and water wall is shadowed and quiet, separated from the city's noise. It is a room for the sounds of water and the fragrance of moisture. The north-facing water-wall reflects the color of the sky and prevents the warming rays of the winter sun from disturbing the thick, blue ice. The north wall is a twenty-foot hemlock hedge.

Access to the water court from the south is provided by a pair of partially walled stairs. Beneath them, recessed sitting chambers offer secluded vantage points. From the north, a stairway directly descends the geometrically terraced slope through a grove of columnar evergreens that heightens one's sense of vertical change.

Throughout the garden, moveable wooden lawn furniture can be pulled into areas of sun, or into pools of shady solitude.

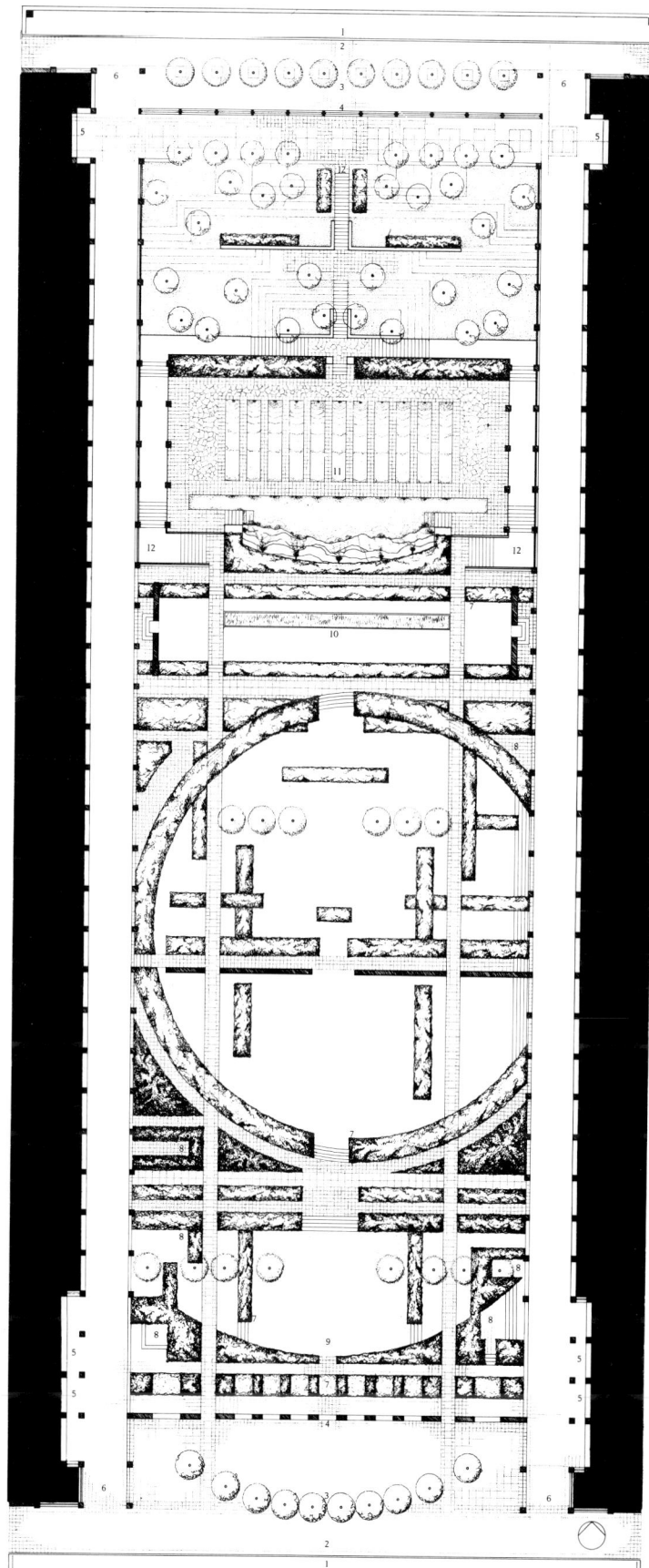

A NEW CIVIC LANDSCAPE

E U D O X I A

1. street
2. sidewalk
3. stylobate
4. screenwall
5. building entry
6. loggia
7. hedge
8. sculpture
   niche

9. lawn
10. iris border
11. ice and water
    court
12. stair
13. terraced slope
    and grove

0   8                                      138

Julie Moir Messervy
Peter Friedrich Droege

Places for Peace:
Garden IV

Having the luxury of choosing any client, program and site for this exhibition, we tackled the design of a place for peace. We posed the question: What environment would make people confront the danger of nuclear war—and help them act to stop it?

We found a model for the kind of action we envisioned in Elisabeth Kubler-Ross's "stages of grieving" experienced by terminally ill patients. Going through the four stages enables the patients to deal with the reality of their condition and take action to help themselves. The stages include shock and disbelief when learning of their condition; numbness and depression at its ramifications; expression of anger and fear; and, finally, action to alter the condition.

Are we not all terminally ill unless we take action to stop the threat of nuclear annihilation? Yet we numb ourselves to its possibility. Reconstructing the stages of grieving may be one way to move us from denial to action.

As designers, we hoped that by representing physically each stage within a continuum, we could simulate the psychological sequence experienced by the grieving individual. We regarded each stage as a

place along a path, creating a journey that would lead the individual to understanding and expression, and thus to action. We now had a program. The question then became: What physical form should such a program take?

Gardens I-III, not depicted here, were a set of early explorations of our purpose. Garden I was a literal stroll garden in which programmed exhibition spaces were set along a path. Not satisfied, we created Garden II, with symbolic architectural forms that resonated feelings about nuclear annihilation, set within a perfected natural landscape. Feeling that we needed a closer integration of form and content, we designed Garden III, placing the symbolic architectural elements within an urban context; the garden journey would take place within a solid block of concrete.

Garden IV, the latest variation, is composed of a system of voids and spaces created by carving away at found places: a park and an underground subway and shopping area. Our principle now was the integration of form, content and context. In fact, Garden IV became its own context: indistinguishable from and continuous with its ordinary, everyday

urban environment in a manner that we intended to be disturbing and unnerving.

To make Garden IV, we assume that a benevolent developer has donated a 120-by-120-foot cube of underground shopping mall space and park land above it for a "place for peace." Located between two department stores and a parking garage, the area is accessible directly from the adjacent subway station. Long tunnels of raw concrete incline upward to a cone 60 feet in diameter; one is now at the midpoint of the cube. Fifty feet high with a 15-foot oculus skewed to the north and west, the interior walls of the cone, coated in gold, trigger associations with a temple, shelter, missile, infertile womb. Gas-fed flames are released through cracks in its walls and in the tunnels. After experiencing the constriction of the tunnels, one welcomes the grand scale of the cone, yet is shocked and awestruck by the flaming gold "inferno" it contains. Is this what it will be like. . .?

Exiting the cone by another long tunnel, one has time to contemplate. Feeling numb, impotent and depressed, one emerges from the underground through a wrought-iron cage terminating at a

one-way turnstile in the city park above. One stops to regain one's bearings: the blackened exterior of the cone looms to the right, and is partially submerged in the grassy parkland at an ominous, strange angle. A path cuts past obliquely. This part of the park resembles the rest, with its open, grassy areas alternated with shady stands of trees. Yet one senses something unsettling here: the outline of the cube below ground is marked in the parkland above by a one percent tilt to the east. It is submerged six to eighteen inches below its surrounds, thereby set apart, made sacred, sunken.

Departing by the turnstile, one faces a large, cylindrical, bronze bell suspended above a shaft in the ground. Stepping up on a platform, one pulls the wooden striking log, horizontally suspended from a crossbar, and rams the bell. Effort is required; expression is achieved. When struck, the massive bell's reverberations are heard through the shaft in the mall and subway below and, above, in the park and throughout the city. Perhaps ultimately, through individual and collective actions, this audible beacon of distress and imploration will reverberate throughout the world.

24

Garden Level

Mall

Subway Platform    Tracks

Subway Level

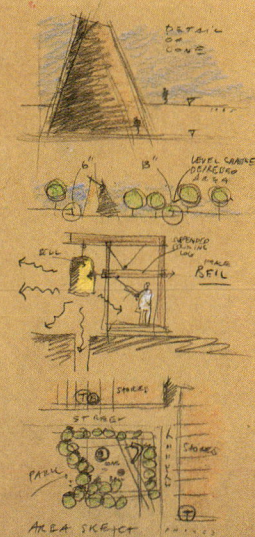

Lee Weintraub
John di Domenico

A Mythological Garden

Every age has its gods and heroes, icons that demarcate and exemplify the limits of our culture. The ancients worshipped the gods of Olympus, built temples to them and engaged in rites celebrating their power. Modern man worships the gods of our time: athletes. We build arenas—"gardens"—where these people demonstrate their otherworldly athletic talents for the delight and entertainment of the masses.

The crowds faithfully come to see these contemporary gods. They are worshipful and watchful, and carry placards and banners showing their devotion to one man in particular—Magic. Magic, a basketball player, is a god of the court, a wizard of whooshes, a man who—with superhuman grace—always turns in a remarkable athletic performance. Magic is a high priest of a popular culture, a mythological figure worshipped by an adoring public, the

earthly epitome of all things Magic.

The worshippers celebrate his power and majesty ritualistically at each contest, sipping the golden nectar of Schlitz and Schaefer and working themselves into a Dionysian frenzy. They chant and scream until they drop exhausted into their seats, and occasionally they fall to the floor in a stupor, unconscious.

After this unearthly scene, Magic retreats to his mountaintop to another garden—an earthly garden of unearthly pleasures harboring the restorative powers that only green grass, trees and water can provide. This garden—for a child of the city—is about an hour and a half by Porsche from the glimmering, shimmering metropolis. Here Magic is restored and revivified. Here he practices his otherworldly talents, unwinding away from the hurly-burly of his public life. He allows the restorative powers of the special garden to wash over him while he wiles away the hours in his Jacuzzi, shoots hoops on the mountaintop and finds release in the lush countryside around him.

The Site: A series of ascending pastures in the horse breeding country of Columbia County in New York

State, flanked on both sides by a mature hardwood forest of oaks (signifying strength) and sugar maples (for color and sweetness). The topography is characterized by a 10 percent change in grade, with a 100 foot change in elevation sloping upward to a mountaintop. This peak commands views to the south and east and on a clear day, the spires of the great metropolis, home of the other Gardens where Magic reigns —Madison Square and Boston—are visible 150 miles away.

This is a landscape of contrasts. A path leads from one pasture through another, reaching a gate where one enters the final pasture in the sequence. The temple complex comes into view about 1,000 feet away, perched above on the mountainside and framed by the forest. Inside the gate the path changes direction, veering into the woodland and out of sight of the temples. Then only the paths and the dappled darkness of the forest are visible, pierced by bursts of sunlight. At the forest edge, the temples come into view again, glistening white and serene against the green of the meadow.

The sojourner enters the sacred precinct of leisure, where a reception area with a hot tub and swimming pool cul-

minates at a statue of Nike, the God of Sneakers. The garden landscape is ordered by architectonic features —pavilions, canopies, trellises—to form a unified composition. Priestlike, Magic routinely ascends the hill to the main area of worship, the basketball court, surrounded by an open temple structure. The pediments anchor backboards on the north and south ends.

In this temple, high above the treetops and overlooking the pristine green pastures, the earthbound Magic vaults into the air— majestic and masterful —intoxicated by the beauty of this very special garden. Here, the master athlete and the garden where he plays mesh and become one and the same—Magic— a culmination of man's striving for human athletic perfection, matched in the lushness and perfection of this garden suitable for a god.

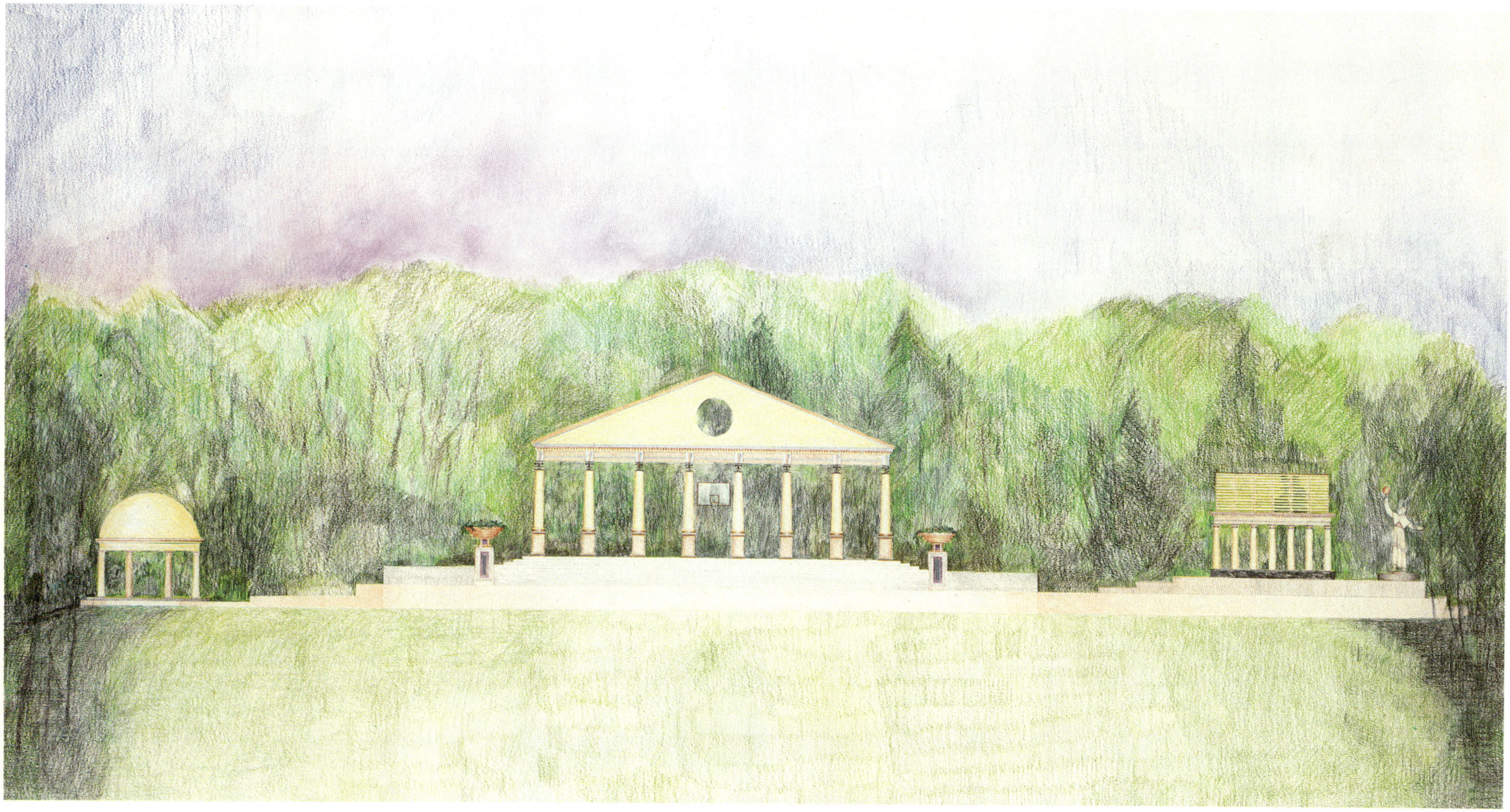

"Gardens always mean something else..." Robert Hardison in *Eccentric Spaces*

This garden is about edges and opposites. It draws its origins from a particular region—the Eastern Shore of Virginia—and from basic, powerful elements of past and present landscapes: the mount, the Garden of Eden, the bosque, the theater, the clearing, the maze.

Gardens are impossible things, really, never certain, always changing. Gardens are about the opposition of forces: a desire to manage, to control, to impose our own order in the midst of a much grander, overwhelming one. In attempting to define a "new landscape," we cannot avoid striving for the ideal, the rational, despite the circumstances that confront us.

This garden is about striving and perhaps never reconciling...it's about being poised forever on the edge. It is

nearly unimaginable now to have a garden so confined that it rules out the world: a pure and private retreat. Yet we still seek these quiet comforting places. Places walled, concave, covered, canopied, human. But they can only be a part of experience, a memory, really: they must let you go, to look down, up, out, beyond. There is in a garden perhaps a beginning, but no real end.

The mount is about aspiration and reaching out. It is the remnant dune upon the shore. We always seek high ground. It is exalting, safe yet uncertain.

There are four pools, like wells seemingly bottomless. Tidal. Dark. There is a memory, too, of a more certain, paradisiacal world. The suggestion of four rivers crossing. An inversion, now a path. Steps down as if you might find a base.

The theater is the start of the journey. It is also rest and pretense.

The maze is a tidal maze. Saltmarsh grass inundated at high tide, channels revealed only at low tide. Seen only from the mount.

There is in this landscape the suggestion of cove, harbor, peninsula, island. The water is drawn inward: a canal along the north

boundary. The land projects outward: a pergola links the garden to the mount along the southern boundary. Paths are by land and water. They compel you to engage the edge, the perimeter, alternately exposing and protecting you. They also seek places: intersections that nudge you outward, seaward. The landscape is about connecting. Land to sea, water to sky.

The garden rooms, walled and textured, pay homage to agriculture: the cultivated landscape, the herbal, the *hortus*, a place of seasonal and momentary delight and sadness. There is the suggestion here of a smaller world, a microcosm.

The Eastern Shore is a stunning, fragrant place. The horizon line. Sky and water intersections. The land's relentless, minute, vertical punctuation and rhythm. It is a place of old mysteries and injustices. Fertility and despair. Where bonded, migrant humanity persists. Old gardens were special, smelling of rose and wisteria. Hanging like the old south in the air. There must be that memory here, but for all a garden's necessary privacy this must be a public place. Like the sea.

There is the relic earth,

boatlike. Trees in cemetery pose. A once and future place. Walled yet inviting. It is truly in between. Neither docked nor adrift. Searching. Old trees like sentinels, gravestones worn by wind. The wind is soft and charging.

This could be a most telling place, really. A garden park donated to the community by NASA officials from Wallops Island. Near Chincoteague. Those who will see this in infrared are still uncertain. Boundaries. Elements. There would be a telescope on the mount.

There are places and prospects here, but perhaps no rest.

The garden begins with symmetry: nine squares aligned. It grows and splits and migrates. Fixed positions that come and go.

Erosion, nature, reflection.

Old places and memories.

estuary

mount

tidal maze

salt marsh

remnant landscape

tidal pools

lawn

iris garden

fruit & petal garden

boxwood garden

magnolia garden

crape myrtle walk

entrance

ramp

ramp

grotto

NORTH

0   8   16        32   FEET

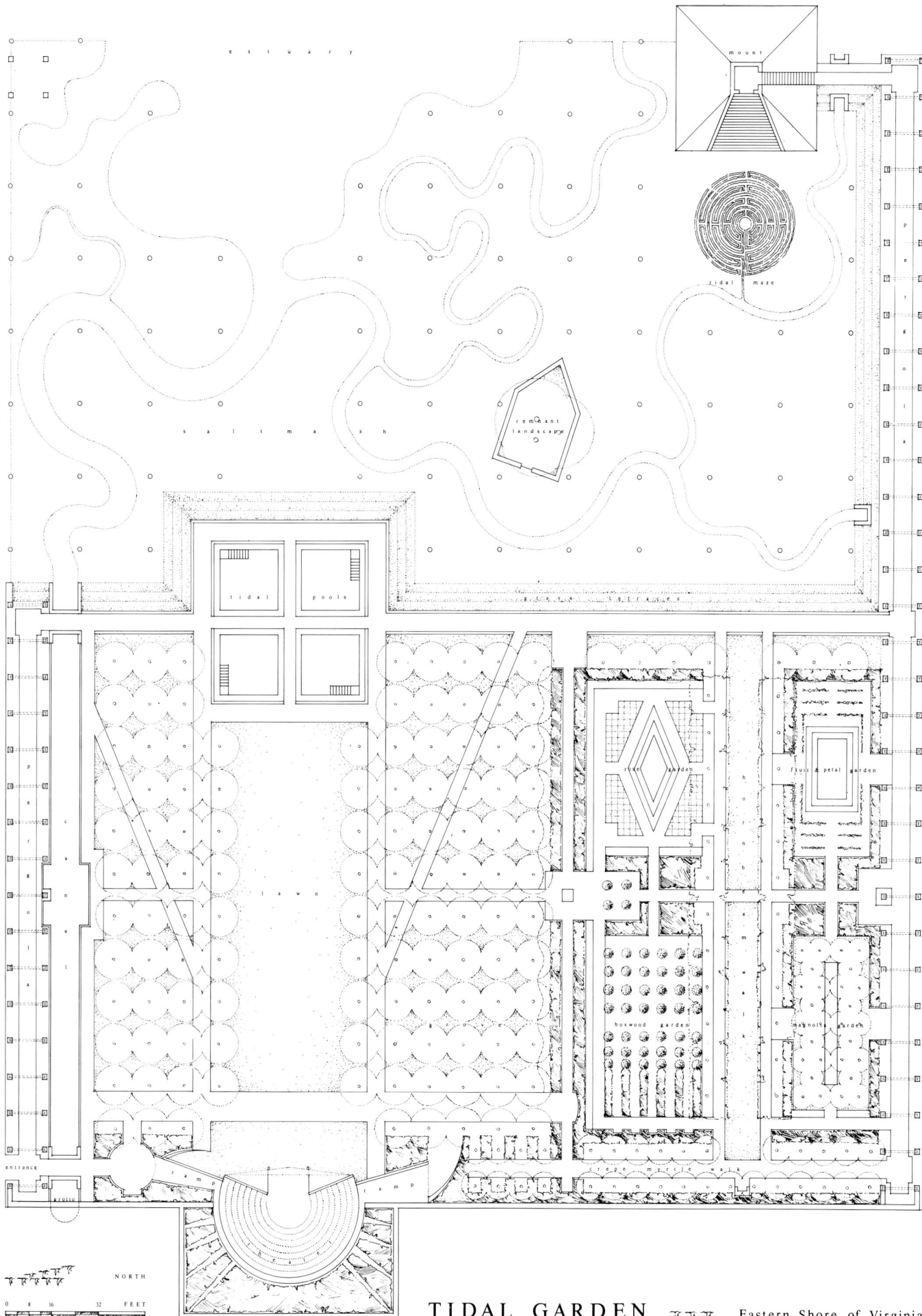

# TIDAL GARDEN    Eastern Shore of Virginia

"The real gardens do not last long—but it is only through them that the knowledge can be truly learnt and people can come to see what a garden truly is."
Abu-Ishak Chishti

Throughout history, the garden has always been seen to represent man's view of his universe. It has functioned as a recreation of heaven on earth and has embodied his perceptions of the universe and how it is related to a specific reality on earth. My garden is related specifically to Persian mysticism in garden design. In Persia gardens are considered sacred and are thought to embody a mystical interpretation of creation. The entire garden and its vegetation functions as a continuous symbol of life and death.

The Sufis, a Persian mystical sect, used images of the garden as analogies or parables in their religious writings. The garden for them became a place of transcendence; a symbolic journey for those who

were on the path to divine knowledge.

My garden is encased in a medieval triptych. The wooden frames, like garden walls, are metaphors of the body as shelter for the soul; the green oasis within. The triptych doors, gates of paradise, are open only to those seeking divine knowledge. The second triptych contains perspective illustrations which define certain important places in the garden. These illustrations are set above a lower compartment which has a series of seven miniature pull-outs, each illustrating an aspect of creating a Persian garden. Each is intended to be an individual story.

This garden, located in north central Florida, was designed for my own use. At the very center of the garden a fountain with a single jet of water symbolizes the origin of life and the center of the universe. At the base of the fountain are four channels, representing the four rivers of paradise and the four corners of the world. The visitor enters from the south through a solid wood door in a blank, concrete wall.

Inside, the garden in the simple gravel and stone space evokes the desert. At this point there is a choice: one can proceed straight to the center of the garden through a

series of eight allegorical gates and chambers, or take a circuitous path that travels slowly towards the center. At each of the gates is a terrace with a different type of flower, representing the eight terraces of paradise as described in the Koran. A series of trellises lining the pathway is covered with flowering vines, radiating out from the center of the garden and dissipating into smaller sections the further one moves from the center—analogous to the image of the onion used in Sufi mysticism to represent the different stages one must pass through on the journey to divine knowledge. The eight cypress trees and eight orange trees along the allegorical path symbolize eternity and fertility. On the other side of this path, four hedges situated in the path of the prevailing winds serve as "breezeways" or "wind funnels" and direct the winds over a planted area of low-growing flowers and into the center of the garden, filling it with sweet aromas. At the central fountain channels break off to the east and to the west. A pool at the eastern end reflects the moon and the stars, symbolically connecting heaven and earth. At the western end a square fountain in a sacred grove of trees is framed by an elevated pavilion facing the central part of the

garden. Two arbors flank the central fountain, reminding one that the arbor was the first structure to integrate architecture and landscape. Behind the central fountain stands the tree of life.

In the lower compartment of the triptych are two chambers with whirling dervishes. The dervishes are used here as an allegory of the garden, following the Sufi belief that when they twirl they become the center of their own self-perpetuated universe. In the center of this lower compartment is the rose, seen by Persian mystics as the most genuine symbol of true knowledge.

The garden is an attempt to reintegrate lost concepts of the spiritual in garden design and to combine elements of the beautiful with an individual microclimate. By studying the mysticism of the Persian garden, we can produce new ecosystems which may achieve a better balance between man and nature.

As a common theme for the exhibition, we were asked to address the flower. Its presence in the garden affects us in both a sensual and a symbolic manner. We sense its color, texture and scent. But we also recognize its metaphorical message of life, mortality and rebirth. Its radiant present remembers the past and foretells the future. Its language is that of the landscape. Its *color* is that of life.

The Landscape/These Gardens

These gardens emphasize the sensual presence and symbolic meaning of the landscape. The colors of the tropics, the rising of the sun, the cycling of the tides, the falling of night, the changes of the weather—all are celebrated. The gardens also mark the transitions from house to landscape, and from land to water and wind.

On the water there is a parterre of sun-blooming flowers wedged in a V-shaped ensemble that aligns with the summer and winter solstices on the horizon. The receding tide reveals a nautical pattern in the lagoon and around the flower parterre. A sculpture of light-columns beams

during the night, fog and frequent rain of South Florida.

The seaside site has three entrances facing west. One entry leads to the house with its patio of palms and pergola. The other two offer waterfront and tower access to friends and neighbors through pergolas and palm allées that mark the limits of the site.

The water-edge ensemble includes a grass parterre and a clipped bosque as counterpoints to the parterre on water. There is also a swimming pool bound by lawns and pergolas.

Next to the lagoon are two lawns. One is punctuated by a palm court. The other contains four palms connected by light-columns to their equivalent of a pergola by the pool.

Our Work

The emphasis of our work is the expression of the garden as shelter affording both freedom and protection; as transition connecting the house to the landscape; as synthesis responding to the indigenous landscape, contextual form and cultural traditions; and as manifestation of memory and imagination.

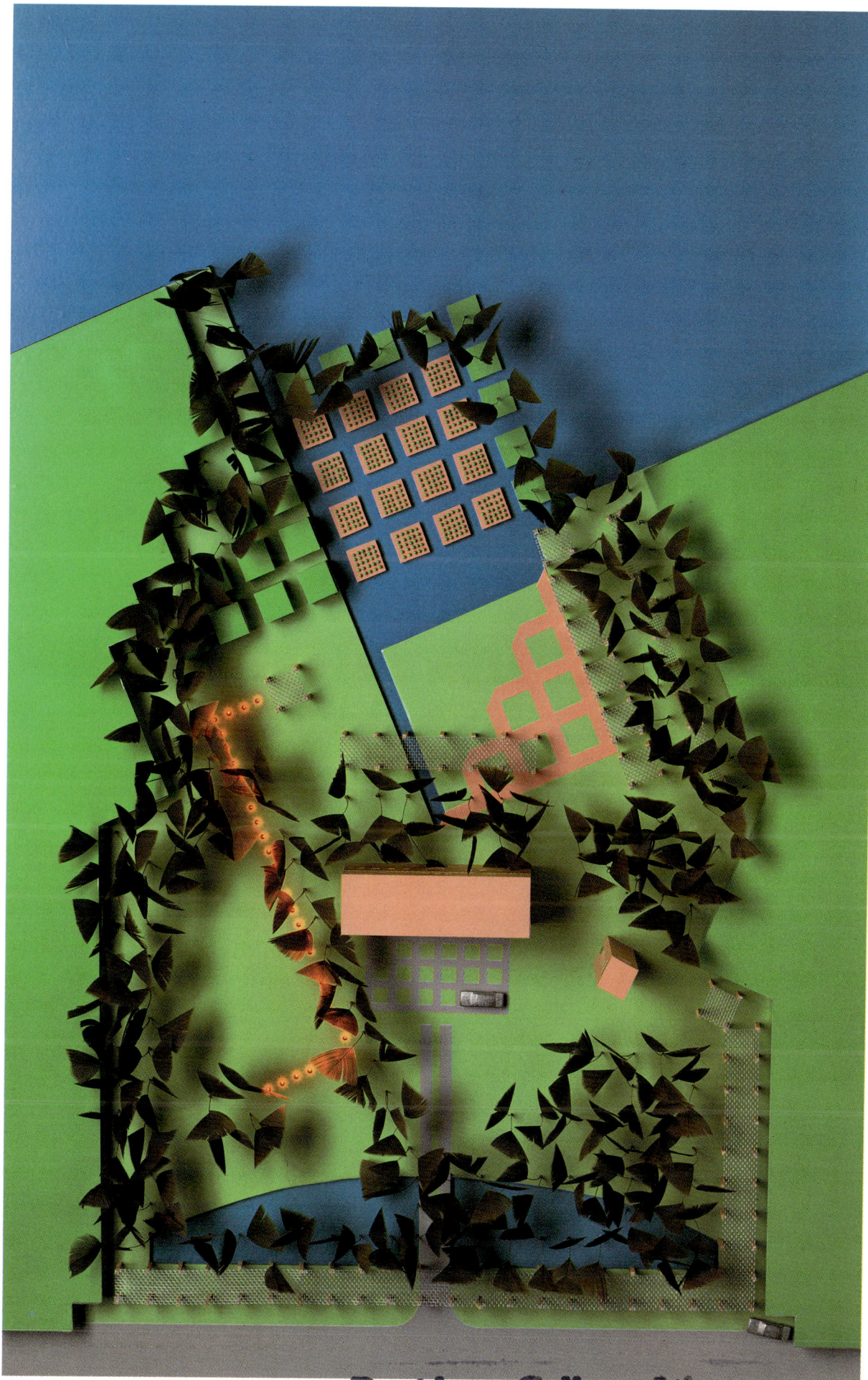

Davidson College Library

An East Central Illinois
Garden:
A Regional Garden

One's vision of the world is a part of the feeling behind—and the subject of—much of one's work. This garden expresses my deep affection for the Illinois landscape. As expressed in this garden, the vision originates in the rural Middle West. The garden reflects my preoccupation with the visual qualities of these places, and my attempt to confirm and reveal them to others. Its creation has required a conscious acknowledgement of the importance and power of both past and current experience.

Living in the Middle West and experiencing its particular light, the expanse of sky and horizon, and the effect of sunset on the flat plane of farm lands—these have been particularly powerful components of my visual sense. During the summer, impressions of changing field patterns have provided experience in spaciousness, incised pattern and exploration. Such experiences have enhanced my visual sense of the power and friendliness of this distinctive landscape.

The goal of the East Central Illinois garden is to recreate the extreme flatness of the landscape—the strong horizon, the essentially open and treeless terrain, the tension between the crispness of edge and the warping of the land plane. The sky acts as an important backdrop for changing light and objects seen against it. This setting and the garden in which it is replicated display dramatic seasonal change at planting, harvest and in the starkness of winter. This is the eye-level carving of grain fields by machine; the asymmetrical slicing of edge, field and distance by huge tractors, plows and combines; field lines changing and disappearing on the horizon in late October light; the visual tension between the empty, harvested field of soybeans and the unpicked field of corn. The patterns are seldom symmetrical, but all are contained in the Jeffersonian square-mile grid.

Across this regular/irregular pattern, the eye continually tracks along the field, road and ditch. The eye either follows the field line to the horizon, or it jumps from field line to field line to the horizon. Although the eye seeks built structures for scale, orientation and distance, the cumulative visual sense is of the entire scene's profound openness. This visual experience requires movement or shifting of viewpoint and direction to reveal the changing variety of pattern.

There are other important qualities present in the landscape of East Central Illinois: The richness and detail of winter trees, for example, seen against the sky. Ground fog of late fall shrouds the intermittent lines of hedgerows. The aspect of age and its effects are revealed in trees and structures: the visual quality of growth originally controlled and confined, but now aging or escaping.

Another profound quality of the region is the directness and economy of its people, and its distinctive places and their materials. There is a congruence between the landscape and the independent, practical farmers who live there. The unadorned quality of plain concrete, metal grain bins and white clapboard siding bespeak an austerity and functional practicality that is visually direct and uncompromising—utilitarian in its economy, austere in its directness.

This garden's purpose is to reflect these characteristics as a visible, built expression, to be experienced through time, seasons and changing light. A change of climate such as the dusting and drifting of dry snow should reveal the region's winds and the variability of the continental climate. The temporary flooding of the front lawn during and after a summer storm should invite barefoot wading. The garden focuses on and celebrates the landscape; it should demonstrate the power and qualities of this unique place. The design sources for this garden are in the landscape itself. The garden and the landscape are inseparable.

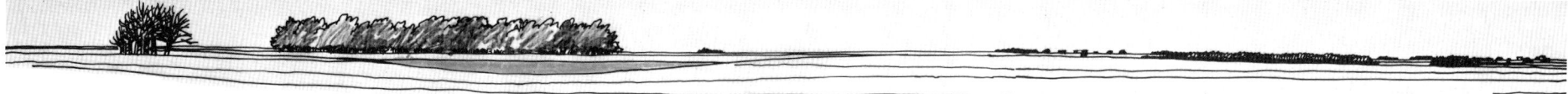

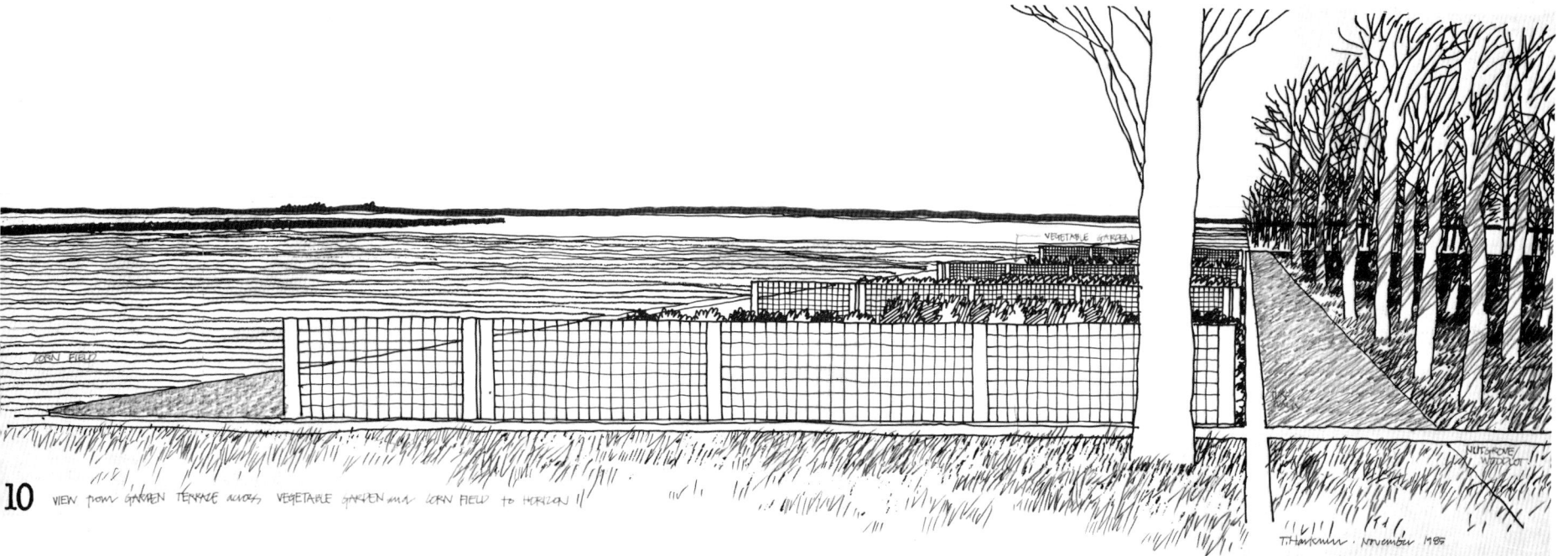

10  VIEW FROM GARDEN TERRACE ACROSS VEGETABLE GARDEN AND CORN FIELD TO HORIZON

CORN FIELD

VEGETABLE GARDEN

NUT GROVE WOODLOT

T. Hankinson · November 1985

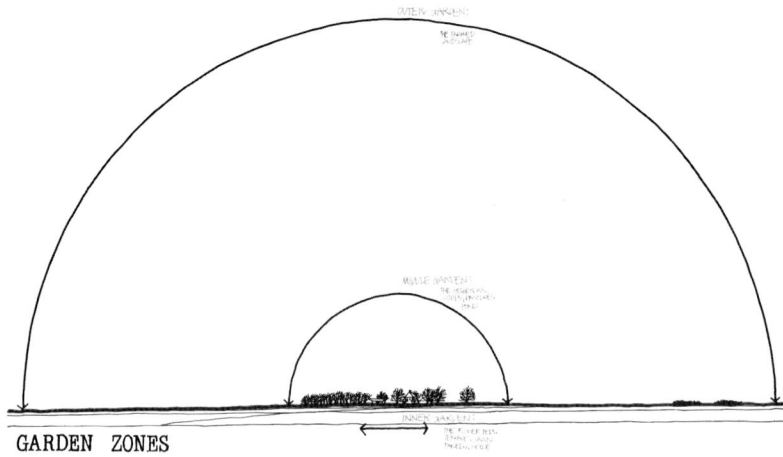

GARDEN ZONES

## GARDEN ZONES

1  VIEW SOUTH FROM NEIGHBORING HOUSE TO POND

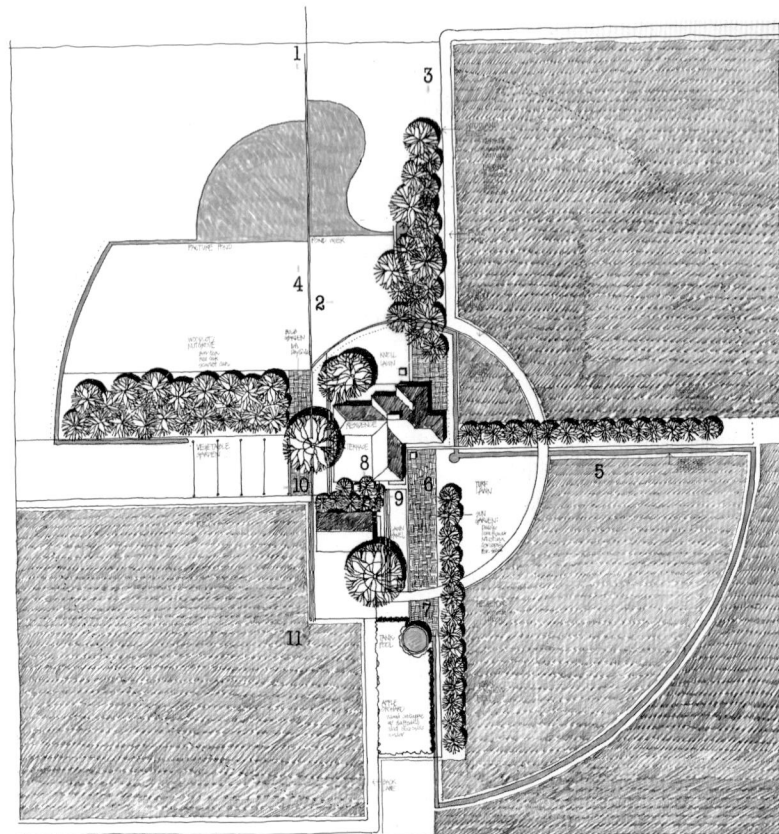

## an EAST CENTRAL ILLINOIS GARDEN

VEGETATION: early spring plowing

HEDGEROW

PLOWED FIELD

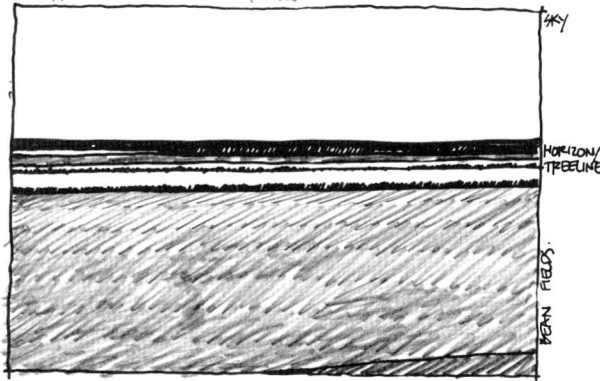

SKY/FIELDS: summer fields

SKY

HORIZON/TREELINE

BEAN FIELDS

FIELDS: fall harvest

FARM

BEAN FIELD

GRASS VERGE

ROAD

VEGETATION:

SHADE TREE

HORIZON

FARMYARD

FIELDS/ROAD:

FARM

SQUARE MILE GRID / TOWNSHIP ROAD

FIELDS/FARMSTEAD:

KNOLL SITE

SWALE

ROAD

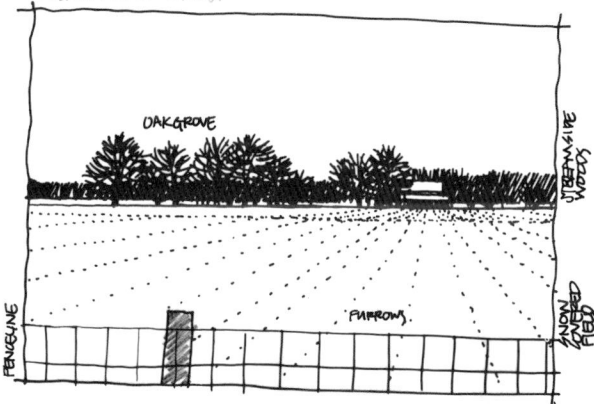

VEGETATION: winter

OAKGROVE

URBAN/SAPE WOODS

SNOW COVERED FIELD

FENCELINE

FURROWS

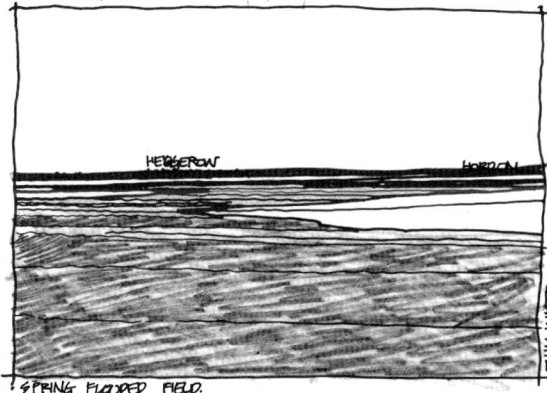

CLIMATE/SEASONS: early spring

HEDGEROW

HORIZON

THIN WATER

SPRING FLOODED FIELD.

FARMSTEAD/FIELD/VEGETATION:

FARMSTEAD

OUT BUILDING

SOY BEAN FIELD

FARMSTEAD: summer

GRAIN DITCH

TREELINE

BEAN FIELD

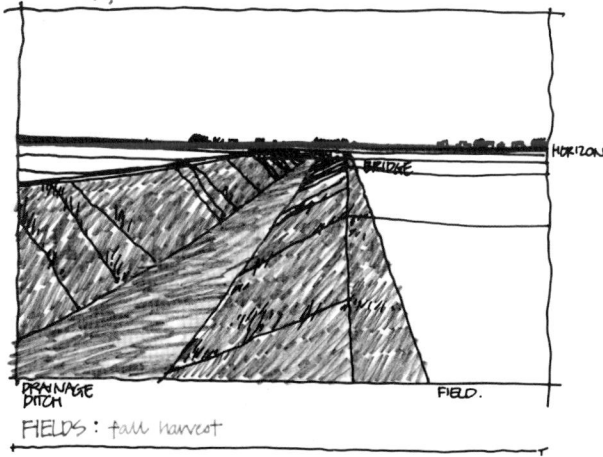

DRAINAGE/WATER:

HORIZON

BRIDGE

DRAINAGE DITCH

FIELD.

FIELDS: fall harvest

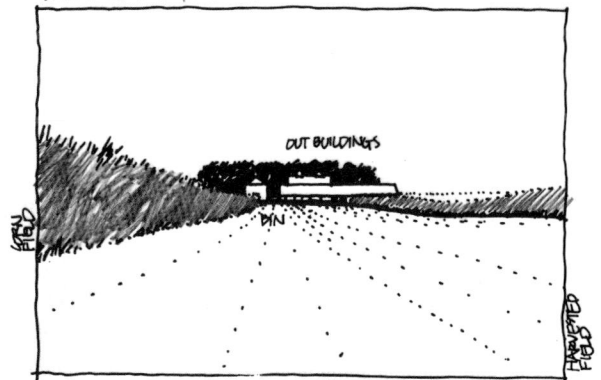

FARMSTEAD: fall harvest

OUT BUILDINGS

BIN

CORN FIELD

HARVESTED FIELD

Barbara Stauffacher
Solomon

2 Fields + 3 Houses =
A Landscape

There is no line where
the landscape stops and
the architecture begins.
People move through
wall of green and glass
as easily as they see
the two with the same
glance.

I have made much of
green rectangles in
my drawings and land-
scapes. They are para-
gon, paradigm, panacea
and paradise. Materials
change. Scale changes.
Here the rectangles are
lavender. Order is in the
furrows of the fields as
it is in the plans of the
houses. Order is orien-
tation and cultivation;
enclosure makes a land-
scape into a paradise;
magic is where illusion
is reality and opposites
merge. A greenhouse is
a garden. A cypress wall
is architecture. A roof-
less room is a garden.
Within a wisteria arcade
there is architecture.

This project has two
sites. If the drawing,
which happens to
denote ideas about
landscapes and build-
ings, is an end in itself,
the site is the five 12-by-
9-inch pieces of paper.
If the drawing, denoting
a garden with three
buildings, is intended to
be built, the site is a
piece of land bordering
a slough of the Petaluma
River where it divides
Marin from Sonoma
County as it enters San
Francisco Bay.

Drawing No. 1

The south elevation
(1 inch = 100 feet) of
three structures: two
boathouses and a green-
house/dwelling fronted
by two flower fields of
Spanish lavender
(*Lavandula stoechas*).
A lap pool segments
the fields. Meadows,
reseeded and luxuriant
with California poppies
(*Eschscholzia califor-
nica*), extend to the
boathouses and connect
the man-made garden
with the meadows and
hills beyond. A triple
arbor of wisteria (*W.
sinensis*) encloses the
site to the west; a wall
of Monterey cypress
(*Cupressus macro-
carpa*) with seven door-
ways screens the project
from the road. Four tall
palms (*Washingtonia*)
announce the
entrances. The eastern
view opens to natural
grasslands and
marshes. Vines (*Ros-
marinus officinalis
"Prostratus," Lantana
montevidensis,
Coprosma kirkii*, and
*Cenothus gloriosus*)
drip from urns, roof-
decks and greenwalls.
The nothern elevations
abut the slough.

Drawing No. 2

The west houseboat and
portico of the green-
house/dwelling (⅛ inch
= 1 foot).

Drawing No. 3

Partial plan of the com-
plex (1 inch = 100 feet).
Elevation (⅛ inch = 1
foot).

Drawing No. 4

The east boathouse and
the portico of the green-
house/dwelling (⅛ inch
= 1 foot).

Drawing No. 5

The poppy meadow
enclosed by the triple
arbor partially emerges
in a boscage of blue
Italian cypress (*C.s.
"Glauca"*), olives (*Olea
europaea*), and euca-
lyptus (*E. polyanthe-
mos*), the cypress wall
and the lavender field.

Set of Five: Two Fields and Three Structures 1985 Barbara Stauffacher Solomon, S.F.

**Pamela Burton**
**Katherine Spitz**

Hydrotopia

This garden in the mountains above Malibu is a retreat for scientists, theologians and convicts. Each personality is intended to represent a different aspect of the human psyche: the empirical, the spiritual and the irrational.

Hydrotopia is a symbolic journey into the subconscious using water as the primary metaphor. Water runs throughout the site and can be regarded as a stream of consciousness. It symbolizes the differences in the realities we face — pathos and ethos, rational and irrational, sacred and profane, desire and death, moral and im-

moral, real and surreal. Water acts as the clarifier and the purifier; it unifies as it distinguishes parts of our existence. Water is collected at various points: some planned by humans; some ordained by nature. It is expressed in various states and its forms include water steps, troughs, chadars, well water, a boiler, a reservoir, a pool, a stream, a creek, a spiral fountain, a water wall.

The mountain is symbolic of alchemy; it is a very risky place. Fire or the absence of water is a necessary ingredient. For some plants, fire is needed to germinate seed pods.

The diagram of this mountain retreat is succinctly described as an isolated circle that is penetrated solely by a funicular, the only method of entry which brings one to the compound's major area.

At the center of this glorious circle is the ossarium, the sum of past lives and a place where the past is stored. Located on the steepest of slopes and covered with impenetrable brambles and tangles of the meanest chaparral, it remains permanently fixed in our memory.

The scriptorium library tower, center for knowledge and the exchange of ideas, is crowned by a satellite dish with a

radio-transmitting device. The base of the building is marked by a plinth of topiary which encloses outdoor reading rooms used by the scholars, theologians and scientists. The convicts maintain, prune and feed the experimental orchard and vine-covered pergola located just outside these reading rooms. Below, on other curved terraces, new native hybrids are cultivated. Water slithers down the curved terrace wall and emerges from a spiral fountain.

An allegorical garden, Hydrotopia functions as a refuge or retreat in which confrontation and discovery are achieved by synthesizing symbolic elements. Yet while the underlying theme is the journey into the subconscious, the garden's imagery is superimposed with unrelated, disparate elements. Scattered references in this garden cannot always be reconciled with one another.

Hydrotopia should be viewed as a series of suggestive fragments that can be brought together as a whole only by those who walk its ritual paths. The garden invites this circumambulation, for in a real sense there is no destination other than exploration and self-discovery through interlocking but not cohesive visual metaphors.

The French psychoanalyst Jacques Lacan has observed that "Discontinuity, then, is the essential form in which the unconscious first appears to us as a phenomenon . . . discontinuity in which something is manifested as vacillation." The discontinuity of Hydrotopia mirrors the vacillation within ourselves. The garden's denizens represent different and fundamentally contradictory aspects of the human mind. In Hydrotopia, landscape becomes something more than a pretty garden; it functions like a language, uncovering through its discontinuities deeper meanings within the mind.

THE EMPORIUM TOWER

THE EMPORIUM

H · Y · D · R · O · T · O · P · I · A

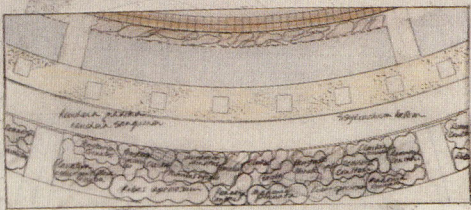

Native Garden Terraces

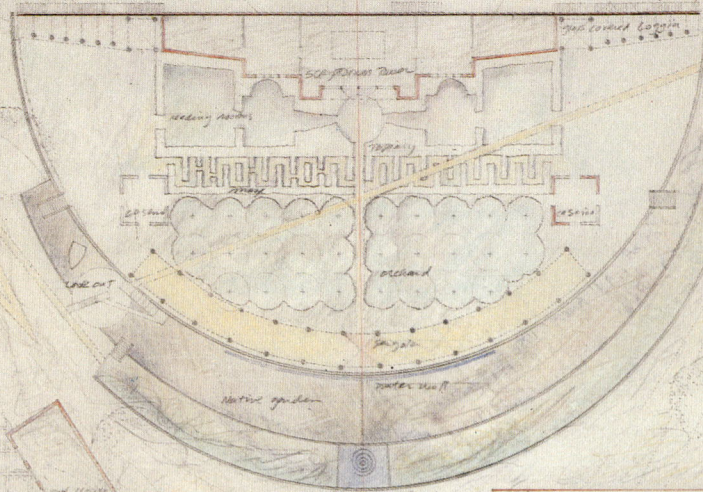

Hydrophilia is a place of water... Water runs through the entire site. It can be seen as symbolizing a stream of consciousness. Sometimes it's wet, sometimes it's dry. This garden is the symbolic journey into the understanding of using water as the primary metaphor. It is the product of scientists, theologians, and farmers. The journey is most important, not the destination. The gardens are perceived and understood through the daily ritual of circumambulation. Water exists in various states: mist, dew, steam, ice, dryness, fog. Water is expressed in various forms: water steps, troughs, chadar, well water, a billet, a reservoir, a pool, a stream, a creek, a waterfall. WATER IS VITAL.

scriptorium

orchard

nave

pergola

chaparral

aedicula

pool

wall vines

element alta

The cypress

swimming pool

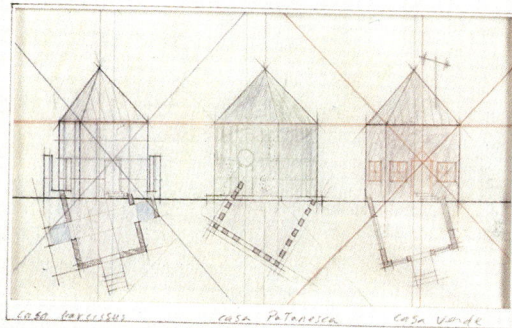

casa narcissus

casa patonosca

casa verde

view from scriptorium tower

The site has at its center a room, the ossarium, a place
where past lives are stored with their hidden secrets. The rest
of the site is a grouping of vaults around this room. It is a...
Pamela Burton and Katherine Spitz

yucca whipplei

The meditation garden of the past holds answers for developing therapeutic gardens in the future. By producing gardens as settings for the practice of behavioral medicine, we expand on the garden's function in healthcare facilities and nursing homes. Our better understanding of meditation garden traditions will add to the role of the public and private garden as a form of preventative medicine.

The Garden and the Senses

Practitioners of behavioral medicine—which includes relaxation therapy and chronic pain control—will often persuade their patients to focus on two or more of their senses with equal intensity as a means of treatment. As each of us has unique perceptual strengths and weaknesses (some of us are more aware of visual stimulus; others auditory, and so on) the garden, a place which can be designed to reach all of the senses, is an excellent setting for this kind of therapy.

My garden proposal contains elements that aim at more than one of our senses at a time, and with considerable intensity:

Artificial pond: stocked with bullfrogs and tree frogs for evening sounds and planted with waterlilies offering year-round color and fragrance

Surrounding area: crickets and berry bushes attractive to songbirds bring rural sounds into urban setting

Garden pavilion: temperature control from radiant heating and bombarded with negative air ions
interior surfaces proportioned and tiled for maximum sound reverberation
aeolian harps in trees flanking the pavilion introduce sound of wind into room
daylight bouncing off ripples in reflection pool adds movement to prismatic lightbeams
at night, floodlights in trees beam off water rather than off glazing, creating kinetic night lighting and turning pavilion into a lantern/kaleidoscope
black, glass-topped, sunken banquet table reflects and deflects sounds and prismatic light from windows
fragrance of incense corresponds to taste of food eaten in room
smoke gives three-dimensional emphasis to colored light beams
wind chimes in trees tuned to correspond in quality to moving prismatic light

Fountain:
radiant heating in pavement surrounding fountain creates warm microclimate at night
fountain's splashing jets emphasize optical tension in tile pattern
pulsing rhythms of the water jet are synchronized with the repetitive tile pattern, creating a mesmerizing effect
high water jet underlit as major focal point in evening
heated, steaming water diffuses light at night and warms immediate area
perfumed water lends fragrance to fountain's surroundings

Garden approach and entry:
Lombardy poplars in flanking rows along the entry path flicker and rustle during warm months
*Cassia multijuga* seed pods sound like "whispering castanets"
in winter, stands of dombeya are in full, fragrant bloom and show through the two rows of leafless poplars and multijuga along the path
shrubs and ground cover flanking entry path produce a year-round sequence of fragrance especially attractive to hummingbirds and butterflies
whistling acacia with wind chimes and creaking, groaning culms of timber bamboo add drama to garden entry during winter storms and Santa Ana winds

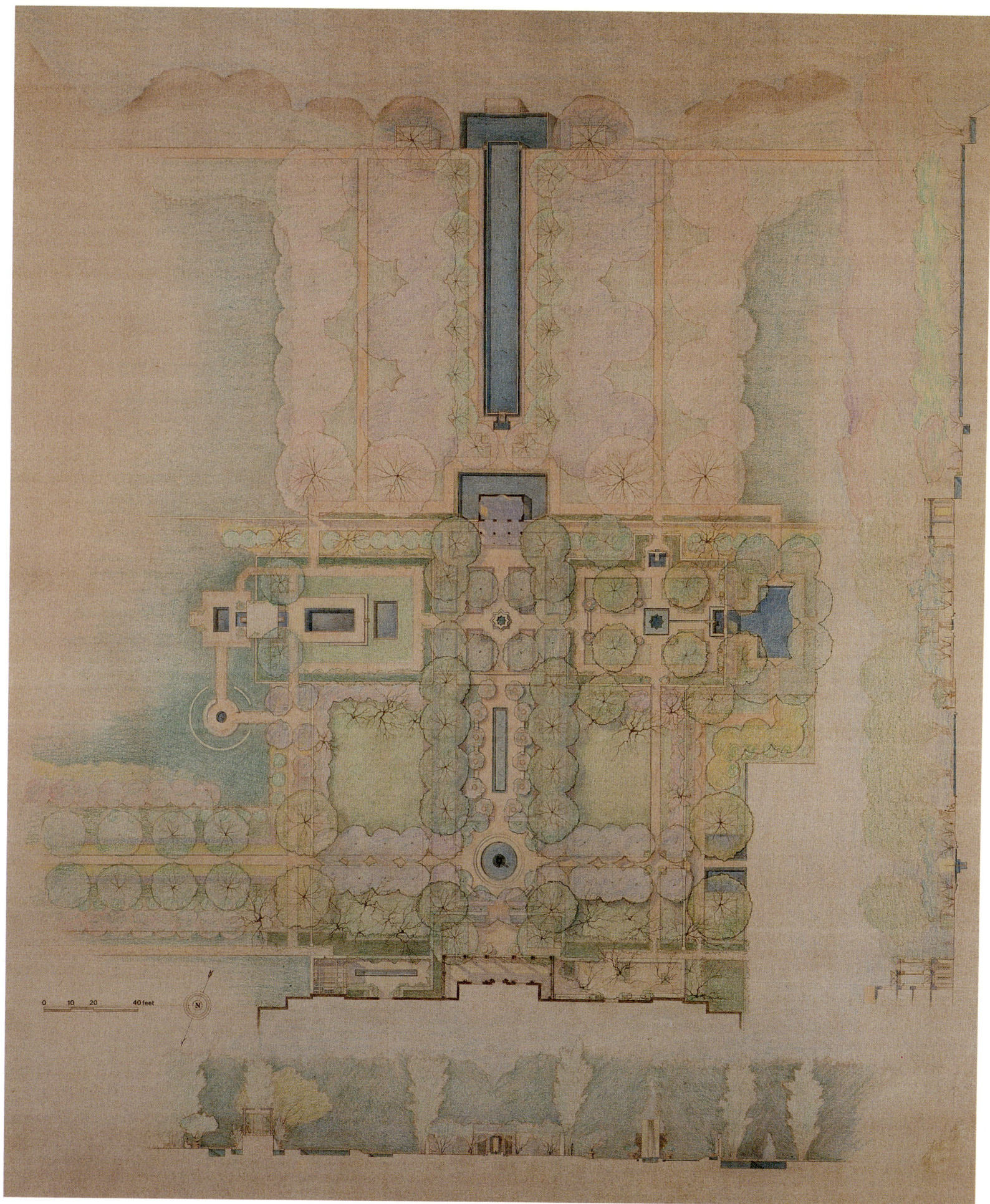

0   10   20        40 feet

Principal of The Office of Peter Walker and Martha Schwartz, New York and San Francisco, Martha Schwartz uses elements not ordinarily associated with gardens. She incorporates them with traditional garden forms such as allées, grid patterns and topiary to create landscapes which draw their strength from the past and inspiration from our time. Her gardens have been featured in a variety of design magazines, and among her recent national awards is the 1984 competition for the King County Jail Plaza in Seattle, WA.

Michael R. Van Valkenburgh, an associate professor at Harvard University Graduate School of Design, maintains a private practice in Cambridge, MA. His particular interest in plant typology and the transformation of traditional garden structures has won him many national awards. Among them are the 1985 ASLA Design Merit Award for the Lowell Heritage State Park Entrance Plaza and a 1983 Merit Award for his Conne Garden. He curated the traveling exhibition "Built Landscapes: Gardens in the Northeast" in 1984.

Julie Moir Messervy is a practicing landscape designer in the Boston area. She teaches landscape design at MIT

School of Architecture, Harvard University Graduate School of Design's Professional Development Program, and the Radcliffe Seminars program of Radcliffe College. A former Henry Luce Scholar and Japan Foundation Fellow, she is interested in relating spiritual and aesthetic ideals in the Japanese garden to a Western context.
Peter Friedrich Droege is a partner of a small Boston-based environmental design firm and chief architect for the Division of Capital Planning, Massachusetts State Government. He teaches visual design and communication media at MIT and architecture at Boston University. His work reflects his major interest in making the environment more expressive of underlying social currents and realities.

Lee Weintraub's and John di Domenico's ability to establish a dialogue with various communities and produce a consensus on design issues has resulted in numerous prize-winning urban neighborhood open space projects. Both grew up in New York City and their firm WD's work reflects a familiarity and concern for the people who will actually use their designed spaces. Weintraub served as director of New York City's Bureau

of Open Space and is a visiting instructor at Harvard University Graduate School of Design; di Domenico teaches at the New York Institute of Technology.

Warren T. Byrd, Jr., assistant professor of landscape architecture at the University of Virginia, explores the issues of precedent and historical context in his landscape design work. Among recent awards, Susan Nelson/Warren Byrd Landscape Architects were part of the team that won first place for the 1985 Cincinnati Hillside Housing National Design Competition.

Chip Sullivan works with Sasaki Associates, Inc., in Coral Gables, FL, and is the 1984 recipient of the Rome Prize in Landscape Architecture. His investigations of the classical garden as a passive architectural energy device have led him to formulate a new design vocabulary. His experimental garden plans have been widely exhibited in galleries in the U.S.

Juan Antonio Bueno's and Teresita Falcòn's gardens reflect a deep concern for their Florida context and their roots in the Cuban-American culture in Miami. Utilizing trompe-l'oeil illusions, exquisite colors and manipulation of perspective, they achieve

expressive designs scaled with appropriate detail. Among their professional honors are Design Merit Awards from ASLA in 1981 and 1983.

Terence Harkness is an assistant professor of landscape architecture at the University of Illinois at Urbana and maintains a private practice in Champaign. His landscape designs incorporate formal spatial configurations with the indigenous Midwestern landscape.

Barbara Stauffacher Solomon won acclaim for her evocative renderings of classical gardens featured in a 1982 exhibition at the Walker Art Center, Minneapolis. Trained as a painter and architect, she has taught at Yale, Berkeley and Harvard. In 1983, she was a Fellow at the American Academy in Rome.

Pamela Burton and Katherine Spitz have been associated since 1982 in a landscape architecture practice in Santa Monica, CA. They design gardens with explicit meanings, using symbolism, historical references and mythical allusions to introduce intellectual themes. Their work was published most recently in *Process* (61).

Vincent Healy is concerned with the garden as a place for healing

Steven R. Krog of Krog & Tegnell, Bronxville, NY, has provoked passionate debate on art and the landscape through his writings and lectures on this subject, including "Is it Art?" published in *Landscape Architecture* in 1981. His designs have received praise from many critics and design juries.

and meditation. He teaches landscape architecture at UCLA and has collaborated on design projects with the artist Robert Irwin in Southern California. As a Loeb Fellow at Harvard University Graduate School of Design in 1984, he worked with author Elisabeth Kubler-Ross on a landscape for a hospice.

Credits

Lee Weintraub
John di Domenico:

Andrew Berger
Billie Cohen
Ruppert Deese
Julio Flores
Bill Giglis
Richard Sullivan
Autumn Weintraub
Shelley Weintraub
Kevin Wolfe

Warren T. Byrd, Jr.:

Model: Jeffrey
Broughton
Rob McGinnes

Steven R. Krog:

Model built with
Michael Tegnell

Pamela Burton
Katherine Spitz:

Jean Bellman
Marilyn Bishop
Florence Blecher
Lanabel Cho
Susan Costello
Richard Hertz
Vinceena Kelly
Pearl Mok
Andrew Passell
Katherine Rinne
Gary Weiss

Michael R. Van
Valkenburgh:

Model:
Julie Bargmann
Cynthia D'Agosta
Pamela Palmer
Perspective drawings:
Raveevarn
Choksombatchai

We would like to
thank the following
individuals at Harvard
University Graduate
School of Design for
their generous help
during this project's
many stages:

Laurie Olin, Willa
Reiser, TenBroeck
Patterson and Mandi
Moerland: Department
of Landscape
Architecture; Betty Lou
Marple, Lisa Green and
Jane Vera: Office of
Special Programs;
Julie Collins and
Susan McNally:
Communications Office.

Harvard University
Graduate School
of Design.
48 Quincy Street,
Cambridge, MA 02138
617-495-9340

DAVIDSON COLLEGE